In the Garden of Fortunes

Poems by

Mark Walsh

LILY POETRY REVIEW BOOKS

Published by Lily Poetry Review Books
223 Winter Street
Whitman, MA 02382

https://lilypoetryreview.blog/

ISBN: 978-1-957755-41-0

Cover design: Martha McCollough

For Harold William Walsh
(1922-1983)
Illegitimi non carborundum

"Nothing's worth nothing that is not seen with fresh eyes."

Bashō
The Knapsack Notebook

First Steps

A birdwatcher's gift   opens over years.

Fortune No. 1

When seeking wisdom
                    Fight for it.

No. 2

At the point of arrival,
your infinite capacity for patience
will be rewarded.
Sooner or later.

No. 3

You are the aftershock of rock slapping water,
rippling in all directions.

No. 4

First Rule for Your Treehouse Club:
To find yourself, play hide and seek alone.

The Second Rule for Your Treehouse Club:
Look for your faults if you never make mistakes.

The Third Rule for Your Treehouse Club:
Accept high praise or awards.

The Fourth Rule for Your Treehouse Club:
Ask fear to Mambo.

The Fifth Rule for Your Treehouse Club:
Hide the Rules for Your Treehouse Club.

Sixth Rule for your Treehouse Club:
Forget where you hid the Rules for Your Treehouse Club.

No. 5

Avoid the loneliness of bus stations.

No. 6

In the slow season
take care: there are
traps in the bogland
where your friend's
love is just and true.

No. 7

Keep the highway in sight in case
your enemy becomes your friend.

No. 8

Oh, Love, asleep by my side,
stay true, for the void is the boundary
of heaven and earth.

We greet the world every morning
with curiosity and hope;
the misty, dim predawn
pulls our gazelle hearts tight,
causing us to quiver with becoming.

Let's share the Afghan
down through our end.

No. 9

The alarm buzzes for everyone
at once.

Fail with vigor; devotion makes
you feel more complete.

No. 10

Like the rising, empty-taloned hawk,
solve problems without throwing blame.

No. 11

In bed
> Better to do something imperfectly
> than do nothing perfectly;

In love
> Don't be afraid of fear;

In sickness
> Every wise man started out
> by asking questions;

In death
> About time I got out of that cookie.

No. 12

No matter where you hang your shingle,

tend your vegetable garden after sunset.

No. 13

After the chipmunk is clasped and eaten,
A diving hawk knows the limits of air.

No. 14

The landscape quiets itself
and comes into focus.

No. 15

A thin pine tree leans
toward your ideals.

No. 16

Viscous broiling asphalt,

blazing symbol with vapor speech
whispering that
every person is an architect
of the future.

No. 17

(with Neruda)

The powerful call of death invited
my many Neighbors, themselves
singing about the defects
of art, flavors spread like
vast towers of Wind-made snowdrifts.

No. 18

After the fire
mark the ashes -
be bold enough to value
each collapse a victory provides.

No. 19

Let revelation surprise you
from the south side of your To Do list.

No. 20

Learn how to separate the rain from water.

No. 21

Your tongue is your ambassador.

No 22

There cannot be more to it than
Obsession.

No. 23

A rolling stone gathers no moss
but it obtains a dented polish.
Roll me over, O, mossy goddess!

No. 24

(*with Neruda*)

The Spanish Age, taut and dry
diurnal drummer of opaque sound.
Now, after the tears, after the soul
master of your cruel ground, your
poor bread, a smile nearly
inspires another. Your mineral fields
extend from the moon to the Middle Ages.
Integrity is a lost essence
unmoved by time. Stone lineage, between the pure
regions of the world, Spain courses with
blood and metal.

No. 25

Oh Autumn! Harkening Autumn,
Autumn of the red leaf and yellow mind
Good news is on the way.

The wind ushers the crisp season
down to your hay-scented doorstep.

Be brave - live wild in the ochre -
linger like air on musty wood trails.

No. 26

Chewed tips of oak branches,
a plunging apple
resonates like pumpkin spice…
There is no reference for beauty.

No. 27

The pitch of your roof determines how
the money is spent, since
action is worry's worst enemy.

No. 28

A building storm awakens the landscape –
To look back is to know gutters need cleaning.

No. 29

The Pointillists knew
an ounce of gold cannot
buy an ounce of time.

Patrons of the Arts take cover!
Do it because you love it.

No. 30

Admire dragonflies on summer fences,
but only in the afternoon.

Rebellious flight, borne on quadruple wings,
sends happy warnings through
the decades.

A girl with a dragonfly tattoo,
a single soul
dwelling in two bodies,
sets space for resolve.

In peace, let dragonflies float through difference.

In New England, not all patriots are dragonflies.

No. 31

A pine tree is a fine thing
in December: Success
is to be yourself.

Has there only ever been
one winter?

No. 32

Sea turtles, under obsidian domes,
cut salty trails inside currents.
They have braved desperate frigates,
left lonely beaches. Never hesitating.
Never too old, too scared, too dead
to hope above the floor of the world.

No. 33

A new wardrobe brings deep joy
but cannot deliver
the glamor of a roebuck beneath cool,
northern mountains.

No. 34

Maybe happiness is more than trying to grasp water.

No. 35

Ten-thousand daffodils dance
over the lightning-scorched ground.

the heaviest task you can ever
                              accomplish
                is to wear it lightly.

Hope that the way you feel
            after making someone you love cry
never leaves you.

In a world of Keith Moons
            be Charlie Watts.

Found Fortune No. 36

Joseph Brodsky!
My first alarm bell,
I sing to your discarded cigarette filters,
your broken samovar, your Brooklyn cafes.

Charles Bukowski!
My mirror of failure,
I sing to your bowery, your handicapping
algebra, your San Pedro lifestyle.
I call to you from
out the vagueness of eternity, imploring
you not to try.

Richard Hugo!
My symphony of resemblance,
I sing to your overworked Duwamish,
to your Chevrolet miles
and the taverns you
have forsaken to save one year.

Man's mind, stretched by new ideas,
never retakes original shape.

O my deities, sing.

No. 37

Along the border, edged in hope,
meaning waits for you.

No. 38

Courtesy is the password of
the grim hour.

No. 39

A woodpecker's knock is hard to answer;
maintain a low profile for now,
since the bug-mad
bird pecks and pounds closer to your heart.

No. 40

On bare June ground
the chick knows a hawk's shadow
and scurries under coop.

No. 41

I don't go to the Pioneer Chicken Stand any more.
Carmelita, betrayed by too much, is long gone.
We can't dance along the pollen path when it rains.

No. 42

A resolution is scheduled death.
The evening zombies
devour their worth.

No. 43

I watched angels
from inside my eyelids.
They smiled and made me alive.

How to See Angels Now

You've put it off too long.
Go out and meet your landscape.

Acknowledgements

A word of thanks to *The Beatnik Cowboy* (thebeatnikcowboy.com) for publishing an earlier, altered version of Fortune No. 36.

I would like to thank Cynthia Bracket-Vincent, Barbara Siegel Carlson, Lisa Sullivan, Miriam O'Neal, Phillip Hasouris and Dzvinia Orlowsky for reading and providing important feedback on the poems collected here. Thanks also to Miriam O'Neal, Wayne-Daniel Berard & Sara Letourneau, and Paul Szlosek & Ron Whittle for the respective poetry series they host which gave me the opportunity to read early versions of these poems in front of an audience. Another round of thanks to my chums John Holgerson, Betsy Hinchey & Brian Mosher from The Uncommon Writers Group. Every creative person needs encouragement, and I give my thanks to Gary Goshgarian, Faye Ringel & Stephen Deblos for their support. I owe a profound debt of gratitude to Eileen Cleary, for her editorial wisdom and for saying that one thing to me that I could never say to myself. Finally, undying love for my best friend, my dance partner and the woman who puts steam in my step, Maryellen Walsh. All my fortune is found in you.

Note

The two poems attributed (with Neruda) (No. 17 from "The Heights of Machu Picchu" & No. 24 from "How Spain Was") are a blend of my feeble translations of fragments of Pablo Neruda poems with my lines mixed in.

Photo By Maryellen Walsh

Mark Walsh is an English professor at
Massasoit Community College, where
he teaches literature and philosophy.
He is a submissions reader for *The Lily
Poetry Review,* and his book reviews have
appeared in the *Lily Poetry Review* and
Solstice. His poetry is published in *Beatnick
Cowboy, Lily Poetry Review, Abandoned
Mine* and *Rituals.*

Printed in the USA
CPSIA information can be obtained
at www.ICGtesting.com
CBHW080522200724
11851CB00020B/775